Word Droppings

Margo Miller

India | USA | UK

Presentation by *BookLeaf Publishing*

Web: www.bookleafpub.com

E-mail: info@bookleafpub.com

ISBN: 9789360945442

First edition 2024

ACKNOWLEDGEMENT

Thanks to my family and friends for their encouragement.

Leaving

In the Fall when the leaves start to turn,
I start my countdown to Winter.
I love the sights of Autumn; the gold and red
and caramel colors swirling in invisible eddies.
I love to see the leaves float to the ground.
And when the trees finally become bare
and the pale sunlight peeks through the thin
branches
I know that Winter is not far behind.
I love the Fall but it is only a passage, a pathway
to another season.
Fall can not be an end to itself.
It can only mark time between Summer and
Winter by throwing off
its garments and running naked through October.
Fall is a flash of color but it always fades to the
bright white of winter.

Withering Sunflowers

Why do you hang your head so low? Why are
your leaves like lace
and your petals tinged with burnt umber?
Did the sun not shine or the rain not fall?
Did you not breathe in the wind and exhale gold
and yellow?
Remember what has been.
What you once were and not what you have
become.
In the beginning you grew through the black
dirt, a small green shoot.
You pushed always upward and during the day
you faced the sun
and your face became like it.
Facing the sun gave you your name.
Remember your name and look at the sun once
again.
Do not hang your head so low.
Remember your bright green leaves on the
slender stalk that
balanced your bright face.
And the seeds that you have scattered.
They will go back into that black dirt and the
rain and the sun
will come in equal parts to nourish them.

And they will grow and be bright
and then become old and like you,
they will take their place in the earth,
as we all must.

Rainbow

Have you ever wondered about rainbows?
Why is the light broken into just those visible
colors?
The rain is a prism and throws the colors over its
shoulder where it
falls like dripping paint
creating infinite degrees of color.
Hues that we can see and breathe and love.
Colors we use in our everyday lives.
Colors that heal and colors that curse.
All from a drop or two of water suspended
in the air with sunlight passing through
and then undergoing a miraculous revision.
A deconstructed ray of light.
For some, a promise made and sealed.
For other a harbinger of hope.
And others, still, a playground of delight.
Light, broken is more beautiful.
Surely we can be as beautiful as rainbows in our
most broken state.

The Crows

As the sun rises above the pale mountain peaks,
a single bird appear in the distance.
Joined by ever increasing numbers,
the crows have awakened from their communal
slumber and have taken flight
to start the bright day with a hunt.
The noisy cries break the morning silence.
A murderous cloud passes over me
and I reach up to touch dark tail feathers
but they are out of reach.
The crows bring omens of good fortune,
the transformation of the day,
the tidings of a better future.
They are bearers of wisdom and wit.
How magnificent to see the unending stream of
ebony flowing from the center of the rising sun.
They fly to the west to announce the day's
beginning.
They fly to live and then to die.
They are harbingers of change, for good or ill.
And in the evening they regroup and return to
the waiting roost
to join the corvid congregation,
tucking their heads under their wings
and waiting in silence for the new day.

The Fisherman's Wife

That old fisherman knew the meaning of
contentment.
The air clear and warm, the sea calm and blue
and his net full
or empty.
And when the flounder, imprisoned by this same
net,
gazed at the old man with those two eyes
and pleaded for his freedom
it was granted.

But that poor soul lost himself when sent again,
and again,
and again,
by his demanding spouse
to beg for gifts beyond all price,
saying to the fish, 'I want it not, but my wife...".
We know how the story ends.
The fisherman has his wish for nothing granted.

And I am that poor wife who cannot sleep
her husband's peaceful slumber
nor breathe the sigh of contentment that escapes
his lips.
I will not be consoled with this life nor satisfied

with promises of the next.
I want the sun,
the moon,
and stars,
like some ancient curse bestowed upon me at my
birth
now doomed to wander this world without
solace.

Sweet Memories

When I sit still and close my eyes
I search in the crevices of time
for those sweet memories.
Ones waiting just beyond
the fresh Spring days in the soft dusk.

The nights have begun to warm themselves
and sweaters have been shed.
The children wear their play clothes
and are allowed into the pale evening
to capture light in their small hands.

Bright points of light
dancing in irregular patterns among the trees
and in the tall grasses.
Caught by chubby fingers
and examined closely by young eyes.

Young imaginations seeing fairies
then learning they are living insects
and yet they still retain their magic.
Lanterns made from old glass jars
that blink off and on,
a greenish glow.
A signal swinging from their hands

like an ancient railway light
that marks the coming trains.

But these small lanterns mark the coming of
summer
and sweet memories.

The Monkey Swing

Suspended from the taller of two giants
in my backyard under a canopy of summer,
as sharp as life and light;
spinning and twirling faster than my own
imagination.
I am the dancer, a dervish,
dizzy, devil-may-care,
at the end of my rope
gripped, white knuckled with two small hands.
Ankles crossed, knees and thighs pressed hard
in precise exacting balance.
Mind, intense in concentration;
body, tensed with effort.
I am the creator, the center of all thought,
of action, of life.
A human gyro drawing bright arcs
in the still green air,
crisscrossing longitude and latitude
marking the spot with an X
in the perfect center of my world.

Elocution

The word
should be as clean as bone,
as clear as light,
as firm as stone.
Two words will never serve
as well as one alone.
The word
should be knife-edge honed
so sharp it cuts through darkest thought
and deepest soul.

Hungry and Looking for Beauty

Nibbling at leaves and swallowing angst.
Munching inch by inch and yet never satisfied.
Hunger drives the caterpillar from plant to plant,
place to place.
Always eating and not full enough.
Days which number his life are few and there
are no hours to waste.
He must eat and eat until the very end.

And at the end he spins his own tomb and falls
asleep to this world
so that he can awake to a new one.
And after he sleeps and his dreams are done,
the morning calls and he emerges from the
warmth and comfort of his silken grave
to spread his wings, shake the dew from his feet
and fly away.
Because he was always hungry and looking for
beauty.

Mirror Image

You are sitting where I sit
and I can feel the back of your legs
against the rungs of my chair.
I can see out of your gray blue eyes;
blue gray images against a background of thick
smoke.
I see reflections in an old crackled mirror,
silver flakes falling from the back like some
precious disease.
You, with your sour twisted mouth
puckered with mescal and rotted lime slices;
your thick camellia folds and fine creases like
used tissue paper;
your unwrapped life spilling to the floor
and dripping through the cracks in the broken
linoleum.
You are not me.
You and your sags and bags and pouches,
old leather stretched and heaved up into jagged
peaks and ditches,
a desolate landscape in shades of gray and
umber.
You, with your herb bitter religion and your
crowns of thorn

and bleeding right into my bedroom on moist
Spring nights.
You and your gut full of knotted doubts, regrets
and memories
oozing their silver mucous trail across my
garden.
You are not me.
You look at me with my eyes and breathe my air
so that I gasp
and you beat my breast in sorrow with your
tightly clenched fists,
and your keening soars in my voice.
You paint your pinks and pale mauves and warm
corals on my lips
to cover up your ashen kisses and you tint my
hair
with silver frost as cold as Winter's touch.
Each day your alchemy brings more lead from
gold.
You are not me.

Goodbye

I'm moving fast like a blur on the side of your
vision,
on a northbound course towards a head-on
collision
with a thousand flying insects
who will slam into my windshield
smearing yellow and green guts
in a butterfly pattern.
I am moving like the speed of darkness before
daylight saving time,
toward a cold, white, inhospitable land.
Moving away from this heat baked town,
deep fried like pigskins, crackled and curled,
with the stench of burning flesh in my nostrils,
snorting and sneezing like a wild mustang
let loose in the high desert
thrusting my nose into the air
with my hair flowing mane-like behind me.
I'm in motion, leaving behind no regrets,
willing myself to look only north
and follow the dipper like milk spilt from the
sky.
I'm leaving behind a weird assortment of eager
souls

trying to make poetry from their hum-drum
lives,
running for my life from their twisted lines
and over-burdened metaphors.
I'm moving at a speed that will amaze and
astound your friends.
I am the first one on the block to to be running
at the speed of goodbye.

Sonia's Last Opera

The ancient Persian fairy tale is twisted like the
dragon's lithe body on stage.
Caught between the promise of if and when, I
buy my ticket and find my seat.
She is an ice-cold princess with three questions
and the blood of suitors on her snow white
hands.
From far away I see the stage, tiny images
through the wrong end of a telescope.
Here are the elements of drama; an executioner,
a knife, a gong rung thrice
and three important fools.
The old woman behind me is talking and my
fierce scowl is ineffective so I change seats.
Robed in a river of silk, Turandot asks her
riddles; in a sea of blood Liu sings her love and
dies.
During the third act I cry, delighting in the
sniffles and sobs that surround me.
The hero gives his name away and forcing
kisses, melts the heart of ice.
Afterwards I thread through the maze of
backstage and find Sonia, her face half white
with makeup.

Everyone is happy, the villagers have been
saved, they take their final bows and then go
home.
Her hair dyed black, she says she will not be
back next year, she must go home.

Malabi

Alone, Malabi stood, three tares tall, above the
swampy grasslands of the Sepik River.
Now he stands with wâken masks who spread
their infectious mists, mgglambi,
over the mid-american visitors on the other side
of the glass.
Those goggling, curious creatures; staring;
reflecting his own concave eyes in their convex.
He stands there silently remembering
shotkamen,
the crocodilian scarification of his past,
the bird-headed serpent that swims across his
stomach,
disemboweled by ancient artifice.
Strong, he stood in the men's hut,
reaching up to hold open the crocodile's mouth
and make the wet ground firm so that the village
would not melt into the river.
Now separate, he stands surrounded by concrete
and steel beams,
and still, he holds open the crocodile's mouth
and keeps the ground hard and no tears fall from
the sky
and no winds come sighing through the trees
and no one knows the Sawos' silent sorrows.

104

An asphalt ribbon running up and down
and curving through the land.
Vegetation on the edges
encroaching on my space.
The wide sky and the broad meadows
fill my head with light and colors.
And the tarantulas dance across the highway.
Do not hit them.
Swerving to avoid the black spots as they move.
And then up.
The road goes up and up.
Past the Goat Mountain and the mesas
and the small groups of buildings that pass for
towns.
A few trees at the wide spot in the road.
Up again, twisting against the red rocks and the
gray grass.
Looking out from the road onto the vista that
stretches for miles.
Unseen edges of the horizon.
And up again.
Past caves and boulders threatening to fall.
Suddenly we are on top. Flat and green.
And down in the valley where the river runs.
A race from town to town but this time

we drove through the blank spaces
between the people,
between the troubles.

The Birthday

Today was really like most other days.
It was sunny and mild, starting not too late and
not too early.
He went about his business, as usual.
Taking time to finish up those lingering projects
and settling the details for the future.
He looks in the mirror and sees the same face
looking back at him.
The beard is a tad longer and the frosting
of silver a bit more pronounced.
He goes through the motions of life;
greeting, eating,
discussing, shopping.
He plays with the dog and it brings a smile to his
face,
the first today.
Worry has created the smallest indentations
across his forehead.
Planning, making good decisions.
It is new and good, but he is tired.
Today is his birthday.
Celebrated quietly with a single card
and a motherly hug.
The years have tumbled him like a stone in a
river.

Not yet worn smooth.
Maybe halfway there.
It is his birthday and another year
begins its scouring path across his life.

It Rained

I love to drive through the country and the cities
and all the parts in between.
The glorious ribbon of Interstate that can take
you almost anywhere.
Just point the car in a direction and keep
following the signs.
There is always a stretch of road that holds an
adventure.

This time it was rain.
Not once, but twice.
Pouring blinding rain that blacks the windshield
and the thwack-thwack of the windshield wipers
must become thwickety-thwack to keep up with
the rain.
Sheets of water falling from above and buckets
thrown up
from below by passing semis.
Griping the steering wheel with white knuckles
and tense shoulders for what
feels like hours but is not.
Soon the sky lightens in the distance
and the car pops out from under a line of dark
clouds
cut straight across the sky.

Oh, the wicked tricks of weather.
The playful nature of adventure.
We sleep tonight in a strange town and tomorrow
we awaken and are ready for more.

A New Chapter

When I read my favorite book I can read and
reread it many times.
Sometimes under the covers, late at night.
Sometimes during the day when I'm suppose to
be doing something else.
That's the reason books are read.
To keep you turning the pages
anxious for the next one.

But life doesn't always work that way.
Sometimes you seem stuck on a page.
Sometimes it makes you bored.
Sometimes it makes you angry.

Yet a book changes with each new chapter.
It may even be rewritten if it doesn't have a good
ending.
So maybe life can be that way.
Start a new chapter.
Rewrite the ending and rewrite it again until the
ending is right.
Just keep writing...living.
Tomorrow is the beginning of a new chapter.

Hope

It is a small pebble worn smooth by tumbling
down a river path
and years of hands touching its surface as it sits
at the bottom of a pocket.
It is the shuddering wings of a butterfly in the
brief moment it passes through your garden.
It is the smile of a perfect stranger as she catches
your eye in the grocery store.
It is the string from a massive red balloon tied
around the hand of a small boy.
It is the knowledge that tomorrow will be here
whether you like it or not.
Such is the nature of hope.
Tenuous but strong.
Fleeting but beautiful.
Mundane but solid.
It seems most rare but thankfully, is most
common.

Death

Death is something that happens.
It happens to all living things.
It doesn't care if you are happy or sad,
sick or well, young or old, or rich or poor.
It doesn't care if you are an animal or a plant.
Not even a mouse or a microbe.

But when death happens it makes us pause.
We think about the meaning of life.
The reason for existence.
We ache with grief for those we have lost
and ask questions that cannot be answered.

Because death is so ordinary,
we make it special.

Older Now

And now that I am older I find that I have
changed.
I look in the mirror and I see wrinkles and gray
hair.
But look closer, I tell myself.
Look at how smooth and transparent your skin is
as it
stretches over your bones.
Look how it glows with a bluish light like a
phosphorescent
creature floating in a dark sea.
Look at your cheekbones.
The skin strains over your skeleton,
cutting a profile fit for a fashion plate.
Yes, I am old.
I am much older than I used to be.
I am growing older still.
But how beautiful are the subtle changes
that show this difference.
How delicate and how tender.
Now I am on a journey to death.
And every day I grow more beautiful.

Humanity

The images unbidden and unwanted confront me
as I wake from slumber.
Nightmares of a nation's past learned in bits and
snippets in passing moments.
Not the ones believed when younger and
unaware of human nature
but those stories of the past dug up and revealed
as truth
by ones who risked their lives and livelihood.
Images so mean and painful that my breath
escapes in gasps and grunts.
How could we have believed a thing so black
and twisted and yet
professed the ideals of a holy scripture.
The breath inside me escapes in hisses and I
fight down the rising nausea.
"You didn't do this" I tell myself, and "You
probably aren't even related to these people."
But I know the past is shared.
It cannot be divided among the doers and the
watchers.
We are all guilty if only in some tiny part of our
common DNA.
We share the blame.

How can I recover from the shame and
revulsion?
I only know that if we continue to pretend that
we are "better than that"
while not being "better than that"
we will continue to be inhumane as only humans
can be.